# THE AFFIRMATION JOURNAL FOR WOMEN

# The Affirmation Journal for Women

## POWERFUL PROMPTS TO TRANSFORM YOUR OUTLOOK ON LIFE

CARMELA PILEGGI

ROCKRIDGE
PRESS

Interior and Cover Designer: Michael Cook
Art Producer: Samantha Ulban
Editor: Olivia Bartz
Production Editor: Jax Berman
Production Manager: Holly Haydash

All images used under license © iStock. Author Photo Courtesy of Jonathan Rojas.

Paperback ISBN: 978-1-63878-884-3
R0

This book belongs to:

_____

# INTRODUCTION

My early trauma and grief led me to work in the mental health and education fields. I stepped into my purpose and recognized my power when I slowly began reprocessing and healing from the most traumatic moments of my life. That journey connected me to my passion of supporting others. Through my work, I continue to lean into the truth of my own struggles with womanhood and finding my place in the world.

The course of my life was rerouted before I truly had the opportunity to discover who I was. I lost my father when I was 18 as well as grandparents in the same month and an uncle within that same year. Grit and resilience were instilled in me early on, and I'm grateful for that, considering how my early 20s transpired. Grief hung over me as I continued yearning for a better future and outcome for myself than what I was experiencing. I kept being challenged by more setbacks, from failed relationships to working multiple jobs, having broken-down cars to post-traumatic stress disorder, emergency surgeries, and more significant losses.

Choosing to heal and see the value in myself took time. It was a journey I had to set myself on and one that I wasn't ready to submerge in immediately. As a bitter, defeated, wounded, and hard-exterior girl, I needed time to fall in love with life again by taking chances and being inspired by the fearless women I actively chose to spend time around. A stack of self-help books I've collected since I was 18 also helped me better understand my journey and face my trauma at my own pace. My setbacks taught me how to bounce back quicker and continue to show up for myself. And that's why I created this journal—to help you do the same.

Give yourself permission today to surrender to the process of rediscovering and learning to love all parts of yourself. I hope you're able to connect with aspects of yourself you've left behind that need love and with the evolving pieces that need exploration. By figuring out where you are in your unique journey, I hope you can plant seeds of encouragement and confidence as you go through this journal for the benefit of your future self. This journal is meant to be used as needed and in no particular order—go with what feels right. Flip to the pages you can connect to most on a given day, knowing that other pages will resonate on other days.

Growth is uncomfortable, but there's a reason you picked up this book. We are all capable of healing, learning, and growing with the right support and strategies catered to us. In order to know what those are, we need to dive deep into our relationship with ourselves. A meaningful life isn't defined by the number of milestones, challenges, or setbacks we have but rather the way in which we get ourselves back up and choose to live and love in the present.

# HOW TO USE THIS JOURNAL

We can practice living our truth by shifting limiting beliefs and showing ourselves more compassion using affirmations that keep us focused on the present moment. The affirmations in this journal are empowering statements that you can revisit throughout the day as a way to ground yourself and refocus.

Each section will start with an affirmation followed by guided journal prompts, affirmation guidance, and a practice called Embracing Myself. The guided journal prompts are statements or questions that will help you further explore what the affirmation means to you. Some will highlight moments of strength while others will prompt you to reflect on personal stories or on the people in your life who have had the most impact on you. The affirmation guidance will help you briefly compose your own affirmations. And finally, each Embracing Myself exercise will combine introspective self-love practices and facts that support the affirmation while drawing on self-exploration, compassion, wellness, and confidence.

This journal was designed for you and will reflect your own unique collection of experiences, dreams, and needs and the tools to get you there. Highlight and write notes throughout, and make this journal your own! You'll be asked to complete prompted affirmations—try to make them short and powerful so that they are easier for you to remember. Write your affirmations in the present tense, and be as specific as possible with timelines. Focus on what you would do rather than what you won't do. For example,

"I will honor where I am today by listening to my body and disconnecting when it needs a break after work," rather than, "I will honor where I am today by not taking on a lot of work." Challenge yourself to find other ways of expressing an idea without using limiting words such as *not, can't, won't,* or *doesn't.*

We can't expect change if we aren't willing to put in work and explore the painful, proud, fulfilled, celebrated, and hurt parts of ourselves. Investing in yourself is a mindset. Let's work to make some shifts and strengthen that relationship with yourself. Whether we wish to break generational cycles, provide ourselves with the best future, or reach our potential, we all have an undeniable worth we bring to this world. Let's empower ourselves and lift up others by reminding them of their value when they're down. Disrupt the paths that aren't serving you, unlearn the ways that aren't pushing you to be your best, and become the active writer of your life story.

Keep this journal somewhere special or in your designated safe space. You can even carry it in your bag and use it throughout the day. Pick it up when you need a release or a reminder of why you started or if you want to practice self-care by reflecting on the day.

Welcome to your affirmation journal and the beginning of a new chapter in your journey. You've got the power; in fact, you've always had it. But now it's time to level up and see yourself in a new light.

## AFFIRMATION

*I am the only person who can do what I do in the way
that I do it, and that is my power.*

## GUIDED JOURNAL PROMPT

You are your own brand, story, and person. No one can take that from you. It's easy
to fall down the comparison hole, especially when you're not feeling your best.
Think of a time you were acknowledged and truly felt empowered. What would that
version of yourself tell you now?

# AFFIRMATION GUIDANCE

You bring your own set of unique experiences, point of view, drive, style, and charisma to every space that you enter. In some instances, we shy away from embodying all that we are. You're extraordinarily you, but you must believe it, too.

   The people who love and appreciate me recognize that I _____ like nobody else.

# EMBRACING MYSELF:
# TALK YOURSELF UP

Acknowledge yourself for what makes you who you are and the value that you bring to any space. Recognize your worth, and lead today with that energy. Know that you can elevate your confidence by leveraging your unique experiences and skills to take you where you want to go.

We often talk ourselves down from taking a leap with a business idea, plan, or opportunity because of a fear that we might get lost, fail, or be boxed in with peers. But if not you, then who? Talk yourself up as if you're interviewing for your dream opportunity. Consider what makes you relatable as well as your exceptional skills and values, titles you're proud of, and things that you're working on. Get in the habit of having a 30-second elevator pitch about yourself ready to use. Go ahead, practice aloud in front of the mirror!

# AFFIRMATION

*I am my greatest investment in life. I make a conscious decision every day to contribute to my well-being.*

# GUIDED JOURNAL PROMPT

Seeing the effects of investing in yourself and your development is a game-changing moment in every woman's life. What are three things you have already done and three you would like to do to invest in your growth and healing? Examples: a service, product, daily action, lifestyle change, or social circle reset.

# AFFIRMATION GUIDANCE

Investing in your best self is a tailored experience and commitment. The drive to invest in ourselves comes from being inspired by others, going through tough periods in our lives, and recognizing that we want more for ourselves.

The part of my life that I currently want to invest in the most is _____

_____

_____

_____

_____

_____.

# EMBRACING MYSELF: INVESTMENT PROPOSAL

Sometimes we can put off helping ourselves because it costs money. Are there any personal investments you've delayed or dismissed because of their cost? Perhaps you've thought about making changes to your space, signing up for a course or membership, seeing a therapist, starting a business, or moving into the city. Investing in your future self means making changes with a focused goal to elevate yourself and reach your potential. To help yourself make a wise investment, consider the following questions:

**AWARENESS:** What is bringing me back to this idea?

**PURPOSE:** What value can this add to my life?

**FUNDS:** Am I able to afford my investment by working out a plan, gradually saving for it, or borrowing?

**ACCOUNTABILITY:** Can I dedicate sufficient time to this? If not, how can I?

## AFFIRMATION

*My voice matters—I will speak my truth, and I will be okay despite the different opinions that may arise.*

## GUIDED JOURNAL PROMPT

To feel silenced and not heard can be damaging. Think of all the times you felt silenced as a young person and even as an adult. What weren't people hearing or seeing that you needed them to? What words would your inner warrior use to validate you?

_____

_____

_____

_____

_____

_____

_____

_____

_____

_____

_____

_____

# AFFIRMATION GUIDANCE

Speaking your truth involves bravely owning your story, beliefs, and passions unapologetically. You have the power to influence regardless of other opinions.

I am enough and will not be discouraged by people who disagree with me about

_____

_____

_____

_____

_____.

# EMBRACING MYSELF: ECHOED CONVERSATIONS WITH MYSELF

Our upbringings, toxic workplaces and partnerships, role model figures, and living situations have all impacted how we use our voice. When we've been repeatedly gaslit in various spaces, we often learn to stay quiet.

Get comfortable with hearing the sound of your own voice and practicing until you feel confident. This confidence will help you trust that you'll be okay and can navigate through a situation, even if you speak up and don't receive a positive or assuring response.

Practice using simple mantras. For example, "I am healthy, I am safe, and I am deserving of all things great." Carry this practice as you are getting ready or are on a walk or drive. Become more intentional with your eye contact, tone of voice, and body language, and practice responding to someone who would challenge that mantra.

## AFFIRMATION

*I am not defined by my trauma—my trauma has shaped the survivor I define myself as today.*

## GUIDED JOURNAL PROMPT

Pain can be isolating and make your world feel small. Trauma changes the course of our lives and reinvents us in ways that we aren't always anticipating. But we choose how we want to heal. In what ways has trauma profoundly shaped who you are today?

_____

_____

_____

_____

_____

_____

_____

_____

_____

_____

_____

_____

_____

_____

# AFFIRMATION GUIDANCE

Stigma around trauma can create harmful preconceived notions and blind others to seeing the depths of our healing processes. Our trauma is always valid, and our strengths have no limits.

My trauma does not define me, but what does define the person I am today is

_____

_____

_____

_____

_____.

# EMBRACING MYSELF: PATHS TO TRAUMA HEALING

Many people experience trauma at some point in their lives, and its impact can present itself in many ways during and after the incident(s). We can experience the aftermath of a traumatic incident or period within our body, relationships, choices, and lifestyle. We may not always be directly in tune with what our body needs to take care of itself after the trauma, because we may still be in survival mode.

In *The Body Keeps the Score*, Dr. Bessel van der Kolk writes that there are three possible paths to recovery for survivors:

- Reconnecting with others and allowing ourselves to uncover what is going on within us.
- Taking medicines that shut down inappropriate alarm reactions.
- Allowing our body to have experiences that challenge the helplessness and mental decline that results from trauma.

Is there a path you have started or one you could begin to follow?

## AFFIRMATION

*I am embracing where I am in this present moment. I will always meet myself where I am.*

## GUIDED JOURNAL PROMPT

Take a mindful minute to notice all that is around you. Set a timer for two minutes, and list all the things that you have accomplished this month. They can be as small as washing your sheets weekly, saving money, or making a new connection.

# AFFIRMATION GUIDANCE

Meeting yourself where you are means honoring yourself on that given day without comparing or giving in to pressure that you should be at a certain point. We are constantly adapting and put in positions where we must be flexible.

I will honor myself where I am today by

_____

_____

_____

_____

_____

_____.

# EMBRACING MYSELF: CLEANING UP RIGHT HERE AND NOW

Meeting yourself where you are is an important instrument in everyone's coping tool-box. It's the easiest first step that we tend to overcomplicate when we feel overwhelmed, lost, or off track. By immersing yourself in your current feelings, you can then see where you need to go and how you're going to heal. We need to give ourselves permission to surrender to the process.

Start by observing the space you spend the most time in. Notice how it makes you feel, what it looks like, and if it reflects what you want it to. Take the time to clean the space, decorate, or reorganize it in a way that makes you feel good. This reminds our brain that plans need adjusting sometimes and that, no matter what things look like, they always have potential. This is a good practice you can apply to the other areas of your life where you're meeting yourself where you are.

## AFFIRMATION

*I mindfully protect my valuable energy and time by restricting who has access to them.*

## GUIDED JOURNAL PROMPT

Think back to a time where you felt you were giving your all for the greater good but ended up depleting your energy and time. List three criteria you can use in the future to determine if something is worth committing your time and energy to.

# AFFIRMATION GUIDANCE

No matter how powerless we may feel, we can always control where we spend our energy and whom we share it with. This might involve doing something proactive or putting a boundary in place.

I will protect my energy today by

_____

_____

_____

_____

_____

_____ .

# EMBRACING MYSELF: PRINCIPLES OF SELF-AWARENESS

Self-awareness has a wealth of benefits. It helps you conquer your most challenging days, make better decisions, trust yourself more, and choose healthy relationships. Reflection is key in building self-awareness. We can't possibly know if the energy we give is too much or what our body feels in certain situations until we go through them. We learn and adjust based on past experiences. Using our senses and checking in with ourselves can help us make adjustments to how we allot our time and how much we give on that day.

There are some key principles to remember when mindfully protecting your energy:

· Not every situation requires a reaction.
· Your choices aren't always going to make everyone happy.
· You must adjust when your trust is being challenged.
· Regularly reassess whom and what you allow to access your time and energy.

Which of these principles have you been practicing lately?

# AFFIRMATION

*I forgive myself for the things I've had to do to survive using the resources and tools I had.*

# GUIDED JOURNAL PROMPT

Every experience we go through teaches us new strategies and tools that can be helpful for our future selves. If you could run a workshop for your younger self, what would the first five presentation slides be titled? Get creative with it, and add your own personal touch.

# AFFIRMATION GUIDANCE

We owe ourselves forgiveness and permission to work through any guilt we feel for past actions. You did the best you could with the resources you had. Allow yourself to grieve what was lost.

I release any guilt or shame I feel around

_____

_____

_____

_____

_____

_____.

# EMBRACING MYSELF: FORGIVENESS MIND SHIFT

Forgiving ourselves is important to our growth and relationships. You can't be the best version of yourself when you're stuck holding on to past mistakes, regret, hurt, and shame.

Forgiveness can take time as you go back and process painful parts of your experience. That's tough work to do, but it also feels very liberating. You may notice that you feel blocked or that you have great things in your life but still feel weighed down. Regardless of where you are, you deserve peace. Every day you become more equipped with resources to draw upon, but it's tough to use those resources when we are stuck with unprocessed past versions of ourselves. Inability to move forward in a healthy way can greatly impact our health. A 2006 study by Reed and Enright found that forgiveness was connected to a reduction in anxiety and depression and improves self-esteem, life satisfaction, and overall mood.

## AFFIRMATION

*I am worthy of the same love and energy I am willing to give and may have given in the past.*

## GUIDED JOURNAL PROMPT

Think of a past relationship that ended. What brought you two together? What made you stay? How did this person fill your cup and meet your needs? Which of your needs weren't being met?

_____

_____

_____

_____

_____

_____

_____

_____

_____

_____

_____

_____

_____

# AFFIRMATION GUIDANCE

Our lives may have shifted based on whether others were willing to receive the love and effort we put into past relationships and whether we were open to the love and effort offered to us.

My next ideal partnership (personal or profesional) will have these three qualities:

_____

_____

_____

_____

_____

_____.

# EMBRACING MYSELF: RELATIONSHIP RESET

In the past, we may have felt like we were giving our all to a relationship and it didn't work. For some of us, we may be in healthy, happy relationships and are looking to continue growing and refining our circle as well as developing new connections. Relationships evolve over time, and we can also outgrow them. You'll notice this happens when you become more irritable, anxious, drained, or not mentally stimulated in the way that fills you. This can also be a sign of a change within your relationship with yourself. Receiving healthy reciprocal love starts with us, our relationship with ourselves, and evolving through our earliest romantic relationships.

A 2019 study by Gómez-López, Viejo, and Ortega-Ruiz found that a person's well-being plays an important role in relationship quality, need fulfillment, the achievement of personal and relational goals, romantic attachment, and the development of individual skills.

## AFFIRMATION

*I am grateful for my body and will nourish it in the ways it needs and signals to me.*

## GUIDED JOURNAL PROMPT

Take a mindful minute to connect to how you're feeling right now and how your body experiences your emotions. Close your eyes, and put one hand on your heart and the other on your belly. Reflect on how the emotions you are feeling now show up in your body. How does it feel?

# AFFIRMATION GUIDANCE

Our mind and body have a deep and undeniable connection. Honoring your body's signals means listening to what it needs. Our mood, quality of sleep, energy, and communication are all affected by how we support our body's needs.

I will nourish my body today by

_____

_____

_____

_____

_____.

# EMBRACING MYSELF: GIVING BACK TO YOUR BODY

Giving back to our body may be a difficult concept for some people while others cannot imagine doing otherwise. This is part of our healing journey as well as our relationship with ourselves—the value we place on our overall health and well-being. By noticing what physical reactions are coming up throughout the day, we can make adjustments to better suit our changing needs. This includes being more aware of our movement, nutrition, and life balance and the environments we are in daily.

Merging the connection between mind and body can help us become more aware, insightful, and present. That in turn supports better decision-making about how we move our body and what we put in it. A 2009 study by Gyllensten, Hansson, and Ekdahl revealed those who participated in body-awareness training showed a significant improvement in self-efficacy, physical coping resources, and sleep. Awareness is key in starting to make positive changes as well as maintaining the ones we've already implemented.

# AFFIRMATION

*I am allowed to make choices and changes that don't align with my family members' expectations of me.*

# GUIDED JOURNAL PROMPT

Write out a disagreement you had with a loved one about an important topic, and then follow it with the ideal scenario and responses you would have liked to receive. We can't change people, but by observing how their reactions make us feel, we can start to understand our needs.

# AFFIRMATION GUIDANCE

You might be a cycle breaker or simply evolving your relationship with yourself. It will take time to be able to validate yourself when making choices that don't fall in line with your loved ones' wishes or expectations.

I validate myself when making choices by reminding myself that

_____

_____

_____

_____

_____

_____.

# EMBRACING MYSELF: RESET YOUR CIRCLE

You are deserving of being in environments where you feel safe and welcome.

It's heartbreaking and isolating to feel shut down and unsupported by those closest to us when a choice we make challenges their beliefs or opinions. We can, however, control how we respond and whom we select to be in our circle. This involves validating ourselves and being mindful of the types of relationships we need and want in our life.

Surround yourself (wherever possible) with people who are supportive of your dreams and who you are, and who trust that you can make good choices for yourself. In research professor Brené Brown's TED Talk "The Power of Vulnerability," she shares that to have true connection, you must be willing to let go of who you thought you should be in order to be who you are. Reflect on who you thought you should be at one point in your life. Then reflect on who you want to be now. Does your inner circle support your current goals and aspirations?

## AFFIRMATION

*I can show compassion and hold space for others without dimming my own light in the process.*

## GUIDED JOURNAL PROMPT

The language we use can help us practice boundary setting. Picture a balance scale representing an already drained you who is helping a friend. One side represents you on this given day. The other represents your friend's needs. What's a supportive response that acknowledges them while not weighing your side down?

# AFFIRMATION GUIDANCE

Boundaries are essential in honoring and communicating your self-worth. Our energy is vibrant, and we exude light when we feel supported and stimulated.

I can be an active listener and offer support while protecting my _____

_____

_____

_____

_____

_____

_____.

# EMBRACING MYSELF: SELF-PRESERVATION FACTS

Self-preservation is essential for everyone. But it can be challenging to maintain when our family and friends need support or unforeseen circumstances arise in our work or personal lives. For example, people who are empaths or caregivers, who work in support or services fields, or who are or have been in toxic relationships can often be more susceptible to this.

Exploring how we can each find balance in our lives while avoiding burnout is a process. We can begin exploring this balance by practicing self-care and emotional regulation so that we can be more in line with our own needs. Challenge yourself to be more proactive daily about looking out for future you by preserving your energy. Save some for you, and keep that light within you burning.

## AFFIRMATION

*I am worthy of a beautiful partnership and lasting love.*
*My spirit is eager and fierce, but I remain patient.*

## GUIDED JOURNAL PROMPT

Think about a few couples whom you admire. If they were to successfully create a three-step obstacle course for couples, what would each obstacle/test/challenge be? How would they overcome them? Think about what aspects of a relationship are most important to you (teamwork, communication, compatibility, trust, etc.).

THE AFFIRMATION JOURNAL FOR WOMEN

# AFFIRMATION GUIDANCE

Have you ever rushed into a relationship, and did it work out? Great things take time, as they should. You deserve a lasting partnership that can withstand all of life's challenges and changes.

I am patient and clear with the type of love I need. I am open to receiving love from someone who

_____

_____

_____

_____

_____

_____

# EMBRACING MYSELF: THE ART OF LETTING GO AND AUTHENTICALLY CONNECTING

You deserve to be loved for who you are without feeling the need to hide certain parts you think may be unlovable. Knowing when to walk away when it doesn't feel right is part of our personal growth. For a relationship to have longevity, there must be compromise, compatibility, communication, and shared values and beliefs. When we're eager to make any kind of relationship work to the point where we give up parts of ourselves, we compromise our alignment with our beliefs and values. Have patience, but stay focused on the type of relationships that align with who you are. Take the time to self-discover and connect with parts of yourself you haven't explored in a while.

You deserve to receive everything you want and need in a relationship, but it will always start with knowing yourself first. Reflect on what you need in a relationship to feel authentically you.

## AFFIRMATION

*I let my curiosity guide me toward new prospects that can be stimulating and rewarding to my relationship with myself.*

## GUIDED JOURNAL PROMPT

If you had an all-expenses-paid trip to a foreign country (your choice) for a month, what would you gravitate to once you got settled? Think about experiences, people, and plans based on what stimulates you. Is it learning about new cultures, intimate connection, nature, new foods, or something else?

# AFFIRMATION GUIDANCE

Magic happens outside your comfort zone. Arriving at a place where you feel open-minded yet secure in yourself can be enriching.

A curious and powerfully stimulated me has the potential to _____

_____

_____

_____

_____

_____

_____ .

# EMBRACING MYSELF: FROM CURIOSITY TO CELEBRATION

It's okay to feel curious about new relationships, opportunities, and environments while also feeling apprehensive. Nothing is final, and we always have the choice to discover, dive in, or walk away. Certain environments may be foreign to you based on what was deemed acceptable in your home as well as finances or even your location. Look out for yourself and alter things as needed. Curiosity gives us the chance to take risks and explore. Exploring a new space—whether it's a community center, a local event, or a new city—encompasses asking questions and letting your guard down while still knowing that you can leave at any point.

Allow yourself to be seen in new spaces and by the people you feel will celebrate and accept you for all you are. Think of a place you have yet to go to but you believe would celebrate you. What does that space have that intrigues you?

## AFFIRMATION

*Empowered women empower other women. I gravitate toward women who help me learn and add value to my life.*

## GUIDED JOURNAL PROMPT

It's time to change the narrative about how women work together, because there is plenty of room at the top. Help your fellow women out! What are some valuable pieces of business and personal advice you would give to your peers? Include something for relationships, lifestyle and health, and growing career aspirations.

# AFFIRMATION GUIDANCE

We can't do it alone. We owe a lot of our success to the figures who have inspired us and validated us along the way. Surround yourself with those who empower you to be the healthiest and proudest version of you.

I know for certain that empowered women _____

_____

_____

_____

_____

_____ .

# EMBRACING MYSELF: HEALTHY CONNECTION CHECKLIST

Ever heard the phrase "you are who you surround yourself with"? Dr. Daniel Amen, a psychiatrist and the founder of Amen Clinics, who studies SPECT brain scans, has dedicated his practice to highlighting the impact of our choices on our brain. He believes that positive relationships and the behavior of those in our social circle can directly improve brain health despite our genetic predisposition. Find someone emotionally sound and available in your circle and reach out to them. Here are some questions to ask yourself when you intentionally connect with them:

1. How did I feel before I interacted with them today?

2. How am I feeling during these interactions?

3. Do I feel inspired? Have I learned something new or feel motivated to improve something within my own life?

4. How do I now feel about connecting with others in my life? Do I notice a difference?

# AFFIRMATION

*I intentionally cultivate self-love. When I give back to myself, I see, hear, and feel clearer.*

## GUIDED JOURNAL PROMPT

Take at least 15 minutes of your day today to do something intentional for yourself. How can you show yourself love today? Try not to get hung up on what you think the right choice would be. Do something that will make you feel good inside and out.

# AFFIRMATION GUIDANCE

Self-love is offering compassion, nourishment, and acceptance to yourself. What you do for yourself will have a spillover effect on those who matter most to you. But let's start with you.

I know that self-love is not selfish—it is _____

_____

_____

_____

_____

_____

_____.

# EMBRACING MYSELF: ENHANCE YOUR SELF-LOVE, ENHANCE YOUR LIFE

At times, we may battle with the notion that being a selfless woman who does it all is admirable. Validation of this from others may have shaped how we view taking care of ourselves.

Self-love helps you harmoniously and meaningfully connect in your relationships with others and the world around you without compromising your own needs and wants.

Sarah-Len Mutiwasekwa, cofounder of the Global Institute of Emotional Health and Wellness, shares that you cannot have self-love if you don't have self-care, self-compassion, self-esteem, and self-worth. All four must be present, which means working through addictive relationships, unlearning unhealthy habits that our caregivers modeled to us, and acknowledging that we cannot fully give to someone else what we can't give to ourselves. How would you rank yourself on each of these four based on the last week (0 being the worst and 10 being the best)?

## AFFIRMATION

*I rest and take space to process my feelings and make choices that align better with who I am.*

## GUIDED JOURNAL PROMPT

Can't bite your tongue? Do you withdraw when there is conflict? Finding it hard to be an active listener? In the remaining conversations you have today, intentionally stop and take more time to process what's being communicated, and how, before responding. Take a deep breath and count to five!

# AFFIRMATION GUIDANCE

We sometimes forget to take the time to process how we feel throughout the day. By processing your emotions and the sensory input you receive, you can mindfully respond, build healthy communication with others, and make better choices.

I will practice mindfully responding to others today by

_____

_____

_____

_____

_____

# EMBRACING MYSELF: MINDFULLY RESPONDING

Every day we make choices when speaking with others, whether that's in person, over email, or via text. Our emotions may be heightened in some way that can cause a reactive response because of what is being said or because we are affected by an earlier occurrence. Taking space or even additional time to check in with yourself before responding is a way of demonstrating self-love and awareness when you can't deliver a meaningful or authentic response. This also includes mindfully not agreeing to things you don't want to do or take on.

Challenge yourself this week to briefly take space (emotionally or physically) when you feel like you need more time to process or regulate your emotions before being an active listener, mindfully responding, or making a decision. This is a way to practice better boundary setting that acknowledges your needs so you can better tend to others.

## AFFIRMATION

*I see every emotional or physical scar as a reminder of how far I've come in my journey, and I know that proper healing takes time.*

## GUIDED JOURNAL PROMPT

Life can force us to slow down if we ignore our body's signals to give it attention. It's so necessary for us to be proactive and in tune with our body! What is something that caused you to slow down significantly and reevaluate your life, make changes, and heal?

# AFFIRMATION GUIDANCE

Physical or emotional scars remind us of transitional and tough moments we survived in our lives. Healing is the part we have a choice in, and it's essential, whether we choose to put time toward it or have it catch up with us.

If my scars could speak for themselves, they would reveal that _____

_____

_____

_____

_____

_____.

# EMBRACING MYSELF: YOU DECIDE HOW YOU HEAL

We each carry unique experiences based on our losses, health issues, accidents, and emotional or psychological wounds left by people we trusted. What we experience is exclusive to us and manifests in ways that it may not for others. Even our siblings may not have experienced childhood events the same way we did.

Time can make us feel stuck and counterproductive, especially when we are not accepting our situation or are feeling betrayal or worry of letting someone down. But it can also eventually be a coping tool as we become more aware of how our experiences impacted us.

Healing from any type of distress takes intentional inner work and time, but it's also helpful to have a team of medical and wellness professionals and emotional, spiritual, and physical supporters. Self-advocating and putting time toward your wellness will benefit you and people around you.

## AFFIRMATION

*I attract what is meant for me, and it won't pass m*
*have to let go at times, and I am just fine when I do.*

## GUIDED JOURNAL PROMPT

Authentically believing and manifesting that you will attract what is meant for you comes from a highly attuned understanding of your past experiences. If you had attracted what you thought was meant for you two, four, or even six years ago, what would you have in your life right now?

# AFFIRMATION GUIDANCE

Every year we gain more awareness and have a clearer sense of our needs. The fighter in you will never want to give up, but we must trust the process. It's always great practice to speak aloud what we would like to attract and feel ready to receive.

I attract _____ with ease, and I'm ready to receive it.

# EMBRACING MYSELF: ARRIVING AT ATTRACTING WHAT IS MEANT FOR ME

Being able to authentically attract what is meant for us comes when we release our attachment to the outcome(s) we wanted. This is difficult for each of us at some point in our lives. We must grieve those desired outcomes while also acknowledging the power they hold over us if we stay stuck idling in this crushed reality. It might not seem ideal, but take time to process and feel what you need to. Know that you will attract what is meant for you when you can clarify what you want out of the rest of your life.

Projecting fears and insecurities from the past will only get in the way of where you truly want to be. Instead, refocus and sit with your intentions. Do the work on yourself first to let go of potential blockers so that you can attract and make space for something concrete.

# AFFIRMATION

*I deserve grace and compassion when navigating new and rising challenges that come my way.*

# GUIDED JOURNAL PROMPT

Prep some kind words for yourself for future moments when you may be feeling defeated and are questioning yourself. Write them down on page 74 and then transfer them to sticky notes placed on your desk or decoratively around your mirror. You can even choose to leave the notes around the house like a kindness scavenger hunt throughout the month!

# AFFIRMATION GUIDANCE

Despite any narratives you were told or have had to adapt to while in survival mode, you deserve grace on your journey. You're only human—you're not supposed to get it right the first time.

I give myself permission to _____ when navigating new challenges or chapters of my life.

# EMBRACING MYSELF: PRACTICING SELF-COMPASSION

The resilience that we don't talk about, and we should all be encouraging more of, is showing ourselves grace and compassion without added pressure on ourselves.

We use what we have in order to help us get through, and in doing so, we experience some unglamorous and low moments. Working toward showing ourselves more compassion is a practice and a necessary part of working through new challenges.

Dr. Thelma Duffey, chair of the department of counseling at the University of Texas, offers these suggestions on how we can practice self-compassion daily when navigating adversities and new challenges:

· Showing appreciation for the parts of us that are hurting or struggling.
· Fine-tuning our inner voice.
· Surrounding ourselves with supportive and genuine people whose help we are willing to accept.
· Accepting times of failure as not being definitive moments.
· Noticing when we are impatient.
· Accepting responsibility for our part in our challenges.

## AFFIRMATION

*I determine and define my beauty by my own standards and what feels good for my senses and soul.*

## GUIDED JOURNAL PROMPT

What makes you feel truly beautiful? It doesn't have to be wearing a certain outfit—it could be a time of day, words you hear, a place, or a scent. Describe it aloud: "I feel truly beautiful when . . ."

THE AFFIRMATION JOURNAL FOR WOMEN

# AFFIRMATION GUIDANCE

Set definitions of beauty never served us well. Developing our own sense of expression is a beautiful process. Your beauty is an evolution and ongoing entity that is more than skin deep.

A beautiful woman is one who _____

_____

_____

_____

_____

_____.

# EMBRACING MYSELF: LOVE LETTER TO YOU

Our relationship with our bodies is probably one of the most challenging ones we'll ever have. Our bodies change as we do, whether that's changing locations or lifestyle, experiencing loss, dealing with medical issues, expanding our family, or so on.

No matter where you are right now with your feelings about your body, challenge yourself to write a love letter to it. In this letter, speak in second person. Mention how your relationship with your body has evolved from a young person to a grown woman, significant moments where you felt your best and worst, why you have gratitude for your body today, and what you still hope to work on to better enhance your relationship with yourself and deepen your connection. Take your time writing it. You can display it as a reminder in your favorite space or tuck it away for the future when you may need to hear from that perspective.

## AFFIRMATION

*I trust that not all challenges that come my way are designed to break me. Instead, they are there to level me up mentally, emotionally, and divinely.*

## GUIDED JOURNAL PROMPT

Imagine you're designing your inner warrior as a character in an upcoming video game based on your life. Draw a picture of them surrounded by words and scenery that best describe all the significant challenges you've gone through that have shaped who you are and want to be.

# AFFIRMATION GUIDANCE

Take the time to assess your current challenges. The pain and tragedies we experience often stem from things beyond our control. We truly begin healing wounded parts of ourselves when we take the time to process and open ourselves up to a mindset shift.

I view every setback as an opportunity to rebuild myself into

_____

_____

_____

_____

_____.

# EMBRACING MYSELF: GROWTH MINDSET SHIFT

Sometimes you might feel like you're constantly being faced with challenges and maybe even doubt your ability to persevere. You may be challenged emotionally, mentally, spiritually, professionally, relationally, or physically at times. Switching your mindset and how you view your challenges can help you return to a balanced state more quickly. Instead of thinking, "I'm not qualified enough for that job," you can reframe it as, "I'm eager to learn and offer a unique assortment of skills and expertise." Adapting a growth mindset doesn't dismiss the feelings that can arise but redirects them to a more resilient and resourceful way of thinking.

A 2020 study of undergraduate students published in the *International Journal of STEM Education* found that adapting a growth mindset led to greater academic success because people were willing to take on more challenges, try new methods, and make greater efforts. Imagine if we let that mindset spill over to other areas of our life, too.

## AFFIRMATION

*I am honored every day to be my own greatest advocate. I leverage my vulnerability and look forward to a better tomorrow.*

## GUIDED JOURNAL PROMPT

What is a cause that is important to you and perhaps relevant in your life right now? This can be on a smaller scale (workplace, relationships) or on a larger scale (societal or systemic issues). Imagine you're creating a campaign and are asked, "What are the qualities of a great advocate?" List the qualities you think are most important.

# AFFIRMATION GUIDANCE

Self-advocating means letting others know how they can best support us. Learning to be a better advocate for ourselves comes with experience, reflection, self-awareness, and processing situations where we didn't feel heard. It's never too late to start (or continue developing) self-advocacy!

I act as my own best advocate by _____

_____

_____

_____

_____

_____

_____.

# EMBRACING MYSELF: STEPPING INTO YOUR VULNERABILITY

Vulnerability is the willingness to share personal emotions, reflections, and actions when the benefits of that expression outweigh the possibility of feeling unsafe. Leveraging your vulnerability means consciously turning things that once hurt you into a positive power within you. The power of vulnerability comes when we deepen our sense of self while being a better advocate for others and the issues closest to us. Speaking out on issues close to you can seem daunting, but there is power in sharing—it's freeing and purposeful and has the potential to create change and build connections.

Our past experiences can convince us that it's not safe to share or speak up. Those are often the experiences we can utilize when using vulnerability powerfully to influence others. Finding acceptance and security within ourselves helps us do something regardless of whether it's received well by others. In what areas of your life can you be more vulnerable this week? How?

## AFFIRMATION

*I define my own milestones. I accept that my journey will be unique to me.*

## GUIDED JOURNAL PROMPT

Depending on your upbringing, certain milestones celebrated where you were "meant to be," from acceptance letters to promotions and engagements. What milestones were you encouraged to believe were essential to your worth? What did they signify? Do you still consider them to be milestones, or have you reframed them over time?

# AFFIRMATION GUIDANCE

You are exactly where you need to be in your healing. Create a plan to reach your goals based on the criteria that feel right to you.

The next milestone I want to reach is _____.

_____

_____

_____

_____

_____

_____

# EMBRACING MYSELF: CREATING A NEW NORMAL

Society often defines what should be celebrated as an accomplishment, but this doesn't always align with every young person's story. You may have experienced hardship, had difficulty accessing resources, or maybe just didn't identify with the norm. Not reaching set familial or societal standards of success can be damaging and discouraging to a young, promising woman. Let's set our own standards of success based on accomplishments that align with our unique journey.

Write an open letter to women in their 20s, 30s, or 40s everywhere titled "Us vs. Societal Expectations." Share your journey of feeling certain pressures and being compared to or expected to live up to a standard—at school, in the workplace, at home, or in relationships. Write it with the intention of reaching others who may encounter the same experiences. Speak honestly and remember to include the liberating moments. Describe how you would like this to change for future generations.

## AFFIRMATION

*My gut feelings are valid. They tell my body when to reevaluate and explore what I am allowing in my life.*

## GUIDED JOURNAL PROMPT

Think about how many times this past week that your gut feelings were trying to communicate something to you. What reaction did you have to those gut feelings in your body, and how did you respond within the situation?

# AFFIRMATION GUIDANCE

If you've noticed a pattern of ineffective behavior or unsettled endings to your days, it's time to tune in to your gut feelings. You may need to pause before you proceed. Resets are okay and needed.

I trust that listening to my intuition can help me _____

_____

_____

_____

_____

_____

_____.

# EMBRACING MYSELF: TAPPING INTO YOUR EMOTIONAL GPS

Our gut feelings differ based on the traumas and challenges we've experienced. It's important to get familiar with how your experiences shape your connection with your mind and body. We may ignore them out of fear of upsetting someone, changing things, or not knowing how to handle what comes next.

We must work from the inside out. One of the world's most successful women, Oprah Winfrey, has credited her success to having an indestructible inner life and working from the inside out. She references her emotional GPS as a tool that has helped her make the best choices for herself. Oprah reminds us that we are our own best guides. It's essential to stay true to yourself because you are the most permanent thing in your life. Consider what your emotional GPS looks out for when you're navigating a new space or opportunity.

# AFFIRMATION

*I take steps each day to set up future me while celebrating the woman I am today and am evolving into.*

# GUIDED JOURNAL PROMPT

When you step into a more authentic version of yourself, you might feel uncertain about leaving things behind. It can be uncomfortable and painful at first as you make shifts. What are some things you need to let go of that no longer serve the person you're trying to be?

# AFFIRMATION GUIDANCE

Looking after your future self means making choices and plans that will help you be successful tomorrow as well as in the months ahead. You are an active creator of your life, and you can take daily steps that will benefit you in the future.

I am consciously taking action today to look out for my future self by _____

_____

_____

_____

_____

_____

_____.

# EMBRACING MYSELF: EMBRACE THE PROCESS

We're often focused on the end goal, but what if we truly gave in to the process and concentrated on where we are right now? You can celebrate the present moment while still wanting more for yourself. There doesn't have to be a fixed end goal.

Every day you have the opportunity to take steps to look out for your future self. That could be prepping your outfit every night, signing up for a wellness workshop, redecorating your space, or setting money aside weekly for a vacation.

Keep these six tips in mind as you go through transitions:

1. Draw on your resources, ask for help, and network.

2. Nothing is genuinely successful and authentic without hard work.

3. Pay attention to the messages behind the setbacks.

4. Keep believing in yourself.

5. You might lose relationships along the way, making space for better connections.

6. Surround yourself with people who are going to show up for you.

# AFFIRMATION

*I release any negative narratives I've told myself about what I should do or be.*

## GUIDED JOURNAL PROMPT

Write three unkind internal scripts you've said to yourself, and beside each, write an empowered alternative monologue. Even if in this moment you don't fully believe the empowered statement, you're getting your mind used to a way of thinking that will both celebrate and honor you.

# AFFIRMATION GUIDANCE

You deserve peace—don't let negative self-talk contribute to your defeat. It's your time to take charge of that inner monologue and mindset. If it doesn't serve you, it contributes to you being stuck.

I know that the _____-year-old me would be proud of the changes I'm making today.

# EMBRACING MYSELF: DEFINING YOUR SELF-TALK NARRATOR

Your inner monologue can have a personality of its own. You might notice yourself shushing it sometimes so that you can work through anxious or stressful moments. Think of your ideal inner monologue narrator versus what it sounds like right now. It can be the essence of a cheerleader, bully, warrior, critic, boss, or nurturer or a combination of any. If it's hard to imagine that, think of your favorite celebrity and what it would sound like if they were narrating your day.

Nurturing your inner monologue and reshaping critical self-talk takes practice. Here are three ways to shift to your ideal inner dialogue:

- Reason with yourself and ask: Is this true or likely to happen? Is this how my most supportive friend would speak to me?
- Surround yourself with people who model self-assurance and honest living.
- Empower your inner child. How would you speak to your younger self?

## AFFIRMATION

*I am allowed to change my mind, to want more, and to question the things that aren't making me happy.*

## GUIDED JOURNAL PROMPT

Making changes and getting yourself out of a bad space is so liberating. But it can take time to sort through what needs shifting. Think about the things within your life that aren't making you happy. Do those things warrant a possible change, or are they worth exploring and questioning?

# AFFIRMATION GUIDANCE

You are allowed to want more and want better. Be mindful of those who have a reaction even when you simply voice that you want to make changes to better yourself and be happier.

I am open to new _____

and am _____ that I can make great

decisions and adapt to changes.

# EMBRACING MYSELF: MAKE CHANGE TO FIND BALANCE

It's not a bad thing to want to change something in your life even if you've put a lot of work into it or talked it up to your friends and relatives. We are constantly adjusting to our ever-changing goals. It's okay to want peace and consistency, but when we feel like we're staying in something because of potential conflicts or other people's opinions, it's time to revisit our wants and needs.

Oftentimes, when we change our careers for a better salary, for improved work-life balance, or to take on a new challenge, it is because we want more for ourselves and have the courage to believe that we're able to achieve better in our relationships, families, living situations, careers, and overall happiness. Do you feel called to make a shift in an area of your life at this point that would better support your overall wellness?

## AFFIRMATION

*I listen to my body and honor my feelings about my experiences, knowing that it will lead me to trusting myself more.*

## GUIDED JOURNAL PROMPT

Visualize yourself driving down a one-way road through clear fields or a desert. As you are driving, there are films projecting from the sky showing each memorable, heartbreaking, thrilling, and touching moment of your life. Revisit those snapshots, and drive ahead on this road meant for you.

# AFFIRMATION GUIDANCE

You might find yourself fixating on the outcome of past experiences instead of seeing the bigger picture. But you can learn to trust yourself over time by responding more accurately to your needs with the strategies you've collected. You know now what you didn't know then.

I am learning to trust myself more with _____

_____

_____

_____

_____

_____ .

# EMBRACING MYSELF: PRACTICING TRUSTING YOURSELF

The first step in practicing how to better trust yourself is to take initiative based on how a situation is making you feel and how you foresee it playing out.

For some who have experienced trauma, their body may still be in survival mode where they perceive healthy images and actions as threats. Having awareness and support along the way can help you reconnect your mind and body harmoniously.

Trusting yourself begins with observing the changes in your body, checking in with your intentions, and assessing if you feel safe and confident to take risks (if not, then what do you need?). Do this self-check-in daily this month to strengthen your connection. It may help to write your observations down so that you can see how things change during the month. The stronger your relationship with yourself and your willingness to show self-compassion, the more confident you'll feel about navigating the what-ifs of new situations and connections.

# AFFIRMATION

*I see every closing door as the beginning of new possibilities for me, knowing that rejection is just redirection.*

# GUIDED JOURNAL PROMPT

Sometimes it's hard to find the words or feel hope after a defeat. What were some self-discovery opportunities that came from times you were redirected in life? Create a playlist titled "Rejection to Redirection." What inspiring songs are on that playlist that help remind you of the resilient force you are?

# AFFIRMATION GUIDANCE

Endings, especially if we don't choose them, can feel like rejection, leading us to feel lost. But an ending of any sort can be an opportunity to self-discover or reroute, even if we may resist it at first.

Ending _____ led me to

beginning _____.

# EMBRACING MYSELF: WELCOMING IN NEW POSSIBILITIES

We are constantly transforming into new versions of ourselves. When a door closes—such as losing an opportunity, job, or relationship—we become discouraged. While endings lead to new beginnings, there can be time in between where we might not see the bright side. In order to fully receive new opportunities and see how new doors can open, we have to work through that internal struggle and defeat. That comes with acceptance and reflection.

Surrender to what was and what could be with self-compassion. Accept what is no longer for you, even if you were willing to go down swinging for it. Reflect on your experience and whether it aligned with your morals, values, beliefs, and dreams for yourself. Use this script when a door closes: "I release _____ because it no longer serves me. I welcome in all of the new possibilities and what is truly meant for me."

## AFFIRMATION

*I am meant to be here and will leave my footprint where I can—it's never too late to start.*

## GUIDED JOURNAL PROMPT

Let's dive deep into our thoughts and feelings for a moment. What does "finding my purpose" and "leaving my footprint" mean to you? Can those two sentiments connect at some point? What is the relationship between the two, and where are you in your life with that right now?

# AFFIRMATION GUIDANCE

We can leave our footprint in this world through meaningful and purposeful words and actions. We can give back to others who need what we once did and impact those we care about.

When I visualize leaving my footprint in this world, I imagine _____

_____

_____

_____

_____

_____ .

# EMBRACING MYSELF: STEPS TO MAKING YOUR MARK

You are loved, valued, and seen, even if it's not always communicated to you. Your daily choices indicate how you want to affect those within your circle, your society, and future generations. Before you can do that, you need to feel proud of who you are and all the steps you're taking to make the world a better place for you and those you love. If you could look back on yourself at one of your lowest points and share what you're proud of now, what would you say?

Processing the past and living in the now can help you look forward to how you want to be remembered in the communities that mean the most to you. Consider what you have done and what you can do to meaningfully leave your unique footprint in every conversation or interaction you have.

# AFFIRMATION

*I make a conscious decision to choose myself every time. I am not always going to be liked by everyone, and that's okay.*

## GUIDED JOURNAL PROMPT

Initially, it can feel awful to receive criticism or confirmation that someone does not want you in their life. It can cause you to question yourself and make you feel out of place. Think of a time when you received challenging feedback or were rejected recently. What steps did you take to respond appropriately without losing confidence in yourself?

# AFFIRMATION GUIDANCE

Choose yourself. Loving yourself in a world that holds unreasonable and harmful standards for women is an ongoing practice of self-validation and building confidence. You are already enough by being you.

I'm proud of myself for _____

even when _____.

# EMBRACING MYSELF: SHOWING UP FOR YOURSELF

Your responsibility is your own happiness—it is not making others happy or ensuring they like you. Guilt about prioritizing ourselves and our needs can hang over us, especially if we aren't receiving validation or we have been/are emotional caregivers. Ask yourself if that guilt is hindering your happiness and, in turn, preventing you from reaching your full potential. It's time to put more boundaries in place that prioritize your needs, even if you worry that others might perceive it as selfish.

Showing up for yourself means navigating the possibility of disappointing people. That's especially the case when you're making decisions that will provide you with more opportunities and the freedom you're seeking. It means being able to hold space for yourself, reflecting, and then taking action to best support your mental health and happiness. What are some ways in which you plan to show up for yourself this year?

# AFFIRMATION

*I give myself permission to continue to discover my purpose by leaning into my passions and making bold decisions.*

# GUIDED JOURNAL PROMPT

The trial and error of making bold moves can bring our attention and awareness to what truly fulfills us. For 24 hours, if all your responsibilities were taken care of and the opinions of others and possible consequences were on pause, where would your passions take you for the day?

# AFFIRMATION GUIDANCE

Our purpose is always evolving. The same things that can get in the way of us discovering or leaning into our purpose can be the very same things that ignite us. Notice what feels good to you, and gravitate toward people who encourage you to be authentically yourself.

I define my purpose as _____

_____

_____

_____

_____

_____

_____.

# EMBRACING MYSELF: LINKING PASSION AND PURPOSE

Passion can help you embrace your purpose. Both are ever changing but essential in our personal growth. While our passions can feel fulfilling, they can also feel overwhelming when issues aren't being addressed. Consider what you feel most passionate about and how that began. Our passions and the things that drive us can connect us to more purposeful living.

Life coach Jay Shetty shares the four levels of motivation that can help us set intentions, leading us to our purpose: fear, desire, duty, and love. Fear can be used as an alert to an issue we want to overcome. Desire allows us to explore and ask ourselves why our choices and definitions of wealth and success matter to us. Duty is led by what we have gratitude for, and love provides meaning in our lives. Exploring our motivations and establishing intentions can help us discover how we want to live a more purposeful life.

# AFFIRMATION

*My mind and body deserve to be taken care of and feel whole rather than just having to survive.*

## GUIDED JOURNAL PROMPT

We can easily get switched onto autopilot. Some days we may even forget to intentionally take deep breaths. Pause for the next 10 minutes to do something mindful for your body that feels good, such as dancing, stretching, or visualizing your perfect day with your eyes closed. How do you feel at the end of the 10 minutes? Do you notice any shifts in your body or in your thoughts?

# AFFIRMATION GUIDANCE

Being more intentional with your daily actions from the start of your day can get you out of multitasking on autopilot. Pay close attention to how you feel during things like sipping on hot coffee on your balcony, scrubbing your soapy hair with your fingertips, or enjoying deep pressure on your body from a friend's embrace.

I am more intentional and present in my mornings when I do things such as

_____

_____

_____

_____

_____

_____.

# EMBRACING MYSELF: GIVING BACK TO YOURSELF WITH SELF-CARE

We find ourselves in autopilot mode when we've been pushing ourselves or have taken on too much. Stepping into a more peaceful and purposeful chapter of your life means learning or relearning how to intentionally give back to your body. Allow yourself to feel all of the emotions that come up. Inviting in self-care and seeing the value of giving back to your body can change the course of your journey.

Self-care is a large umbrella of intentional choices and acts that help us recharge, replenish, rest, and shift away from autopilot. We can have ritualistic (weekly or daily occurrences), planned, or unplanned self-care. Nourish your body, embrace it, and use it in ways to elevate your experience in the here and now. Jot down your self-care lineup this week that is either ritualistic or planned. Be open to having to add unplanned self-care to your week.

# AFFIRMATION

*I operate from a place of wholeness, abundance, and self-awareness. I accept the journey that I am on.*

# GUIDED JOURNAL PROMPT

It's okay to feel like you're not where you want to be. Reflect on a few hard truths you've had to accept in your lifetime that you weren't prepared for but that helped you evolve.

# AFFIRMATION GUIDANCE

Working toward self-acceptance is finding peace in the pain you've gone through and seeing value in yourself. Disconnecting from ourselves and remaining depleted moves us away from feeling fulfilled and whole.

    I am grateful for _____ in helping me work toward acceptance.

# EMBRACING MYSELF: MEDITATE ON IT

Today is going to be a beautiful day; you have everything in you to make it so. Be present right now, and remind yourself that you don't have to have it all figured out. Close your eyes and take a deep breath, inhaling for 5 seconds and exhaling for 10 seconds. Notice the sensations that your body is experiencing, and affirm three things that you are grateful for in this moment. Challenge yourself this week to take time in your day to be in a quiet space, disconnected from screens and being present minded.

At the end of each day, you can benefit from taking the time to process the day's events to start tomorrow with a clean slate. Someone else's successes or happiness do not change your journey. Focus on you, and put that energy back into healing. Some of the best ways to do this are in nature or our safe spaces.

## AFFIRMATION

*I know that pausing and resetting is necessary to my personal growth and honoring the relationship I have with myself.*

## GUIDED JOURNAL PROMPT

Sometimes staying comfortable can actually mean that we are stuck. When is the last time you switched up your schedule? Write down a list of some ideas for how you can relax, recharge, and reset.

# AFFIRMATION GUIDANCE

We're lovers, wanderers, givers, doers, performers, healers, and flourishing women. You can't give if you have nothing left. We must be aware and selective about where we allot our emotional energy. Along with that comes knowing when to rest.

My level of productivity today does not determine

_____

_____

_____

_____

_____.

# EMBRACING MYSELF: PAUSE AND RESET

When we pause, it forces us to examine our relationship with ourselves.

Observe how you treat yourself, in which spaces you feel most connected to yourself, how much time tasks are taking you, how you choose to heal and nurture previous wounds, and how much time you spend each week giving back to yourself. Self-sacrificing tendencies, as well as burnout, are indications that you need an immediate reset.

A reset can come in the form of taking space, committing to or pulling away from certain relationships, and also finding focused support. Being part of a community, such as peer-support groups with those who have similar experiences, can benefit your mental health by empowering you to explore new coping skills and learn from others. Declutter your mind, prioritize rest, reconnect to yourself, and deepen your relationships with like-minded people outside your circle.

# AFFIRMATION

*I exude passion in all areas of my life. Good things are coming my way!*

# GUIDED JOURNAL PROMPT

If you could see a passionate version of yourself through the eyes of someone you work with, love, or have briefly interacted with, what would they see and think when you're working, speaking, or caring for others? What does a passionate you look like?

_____

_____

_____

_____

_____

_____

_____

_____

_____

_____

_____

_____

_____

# AFFIRMATION GUIDANCE

Experiencing anxiety and hypervigilance when preparing for your next hurdle is natural and valid. Exploring those reactions can help you shift your mindset to embrace the good things that will come your way. Immerse yourself in your passions while working through what you need to.

I trust that leading with passion in my day can increase my chance of _____

_____

_____

_____

_____

_____.

# EMBRACING MYSELF: EXUDING PASSION

Be gentle with yourself, and know that your passion speaks louder than what you're wearing and what accomplishments you do or don't have. Our passions can be found in our work, volunteer time, side hustles, forms of expression, spaces where we feel stimulated or at peace, creative outlets, family time, and friendships. We can observe them through our attitude, mood, actions, and persistence in educating, inspiring, and sharing with others.

Passionate people are happier and more engaged. If you're feeling lost or off track, reflect on and connect to where your passions may reside. Your passion will radiate effortlessly, so lean into what feels good and right for you.

Robert J. Vallerand's 2012 study found that those who have harmonious passions will have positive emotions while engaged in them, thus leading to increased psychological well-being. Consider the benefits of leading your days with passion and how that will impact the way others experience you.

# AFFIRMATION

*I can control only what I can control, and I mindfully tend to what may be doing a disservice to me.*

# GUIDED JOURNAL PROMPT

What has your relationship with control looked like over the years, and what is its role in your life today? It takes practice to know what you can and cannot control. List five things you can control for certain within your day today.

# AFFIRMATION GUIDANCE

Noticing what is within your control in a situation can alter your response. Being in situations where you are left to resort to bad habits because you feel an imbalance of control indicates that you need to make an adjustment.

I can make a healthy shift by taking control of _____

_____

_____

_____

_____

_____

_____.

# EMBRACING MYSELF: REPLACING UNHEALTHY TENDENCIES

The choices we make and the things we invite into our lives can unintentionally do a disservice to our needs and well-being. These include unhealthy habits, self-sabotaging behavior, negative self-talk, and toxic relationships and mindset. Consider the habits and actions within your own life that are doing a disservice to your needs and the well-being of your future self.

Redesign the life you want by taking action and living authentically. Take action by assessing what in your life is a want versus a need. Can that habit be replaced with something else that gives your brain and body a similar feeling while not compromising your well-being? Ask for help along the way, and find community—this process will test you. You have the power to invest in your mental and physical health, but you have to want that change. Consider a habit you have that is unhealthy in some way. Why do you do it, and what can it be replaced with?

## AFFIRMATION

*I am allowed to ask for help in any capacity. I do not have to carry it all alone.*

## GUIDED JOURNAL PROMPT

If you could run a women's help hotline, what services would you offer? There are no limits—they could be physical, mental, relational, recreational, or wellness-related. Can you think of any women you know who are open about receiving help that you would possibly appoint as spokespeople?

# AFFIRMATION GUIDANCE

Our upbringing and the spaces that are part of our routine can encourage a culture of overworking to the point of burnout. When we're depleted, it can be difficult to tap into our self-awareness and act in our best interest.

I don't have to carry the weight of _____ on my own.

# EMBRACING MYSELF: IF-THEN ACCOUNTABILITY

Have the courage to pause and be honest with yourself about what you need help with in your life. No one can do what you do in the way you do it, but a rested and recharged you can elevate that even more. Communicating your needs is an important part of recharging. You need to ask for what you want—don't assume people know.

Likewise, allow yourself to take a day off—your work and duties will still be there when you return. Taking space can help you tap into your creativity, become grounded and inspired, and see things with a fresh lens.

If-then statements can help you hold yourself accountable. Use the following prompts for reference.

If I'm _____, then I'll ask for help.

If I'm _____, then I'll call _____.

If I'm _____, then I'll benefit from taking some space for myself.

If I'm _____, then _____.

## AFFIRMATION

*I am committed to being the best version of myself and will stay focused on my goals while keeping an open mind.*

## GUIDED JOURNAL PROMPT

Focusing on goals can help you reach an elevated version of yourself. Being open-minded and learning along the way can also be incredibly fulfilling. What are a few things you'd like to learn or are open to trying?

# AFFIRMATION GUIDANCE

Having set goals is beneficial to bettering yourself, but it's important not to become fixated on them without any room for flexibility or adjustment. Becoming the best version of yourself also must include honoring your process.

I commit to _____
as I am working toward the best version of myself.

# EMBRACING MYSELF: IT'S TIME TO STEP UP

Put some value on yourself. Even if your goals and dreams seem out of reach at this point, know that every intentional step counts. Commit to self-improvement and your personal development. A 2021 *Harvard Business Review* article identified that the top three ways to become the best version of yourself are turning weaknesses into strengths, setting and tracking goals, and finding opportunities to learn.

Working toward the best version of yourself requires you to keep an open mind because there may be another way to reach your goal that you didn't plan for. It's important to hold yourself accountable by keeping track of your progress as well as prioritizing learning. What can you do this month to strengthen your skills and educate yourself on your area of expertise or something new? What tools can you use to set and track your goals, such as journaling or using an online organizational app or site?

# AFFIRMATION

*There is no reward without risk. I will take chances and bet on myself for a deserving future me.*

# GUIDED JOURNAL PROMPT

It's human nature to gravitate to what feels safe to us. We may fear that taking risks will leave us worse off than we are. But what if they lead to a better you? Who are some women in your life or ones you look up to who have bet on themselves?

# AFFIRMATION GUIDANCE

Don't let your fear stop you from getting started. There may have been points in your life where the idea of more change was unbearable because of what was happening beyond your control. Now is the time to welcome a better tomorrow, and it starts with betting on yourself.

I choose to bet on myself by _____

_____

_____

_____

_____

_____.

# EMBRACING MYSELF: VISUALIZATION FOR YOUR INNER RISK-TAKER

This is your year to show everyone who you are. While it's important to never forget how far we've come, we must reflect on what is holding us back when we have a new idea or when we feel called to a new location, venture, or relationship. Is it fear, self-doubt, unprocessed pain from the past, or a particular someone? What's making you want to lean in? Is it wanting more for yourself, proving your capabilities to others, or genuinely wanting to create the peace that you haven't been able to find?

Get in the practice of visualizing your next big move daily—the progress and the outcome. Close your eyes, and picture how your life could ideally look after you bet on yourself. Who do you see being around you and celebrating you? Use music, movies, sports montages, and podcasts that inspire you when visualizing. Take a chance on yourself.

# RESOURCES

**Headspace app**
A great daily tool that offers videos, audio, and guides for meditation, sleep, and movement.

**PsychologyToday.com**
A mental health support hub with articles and information (personal growth, relationships, mental health, etc.) where you can also find a local therapist who fits your needs.

***Super Soul* Oprah Winfrey podcast**
Provides inspiration for becoming your best self via the stories and practices of health and wellness experts as well as some successful people who have faced adversity.

***Unlocking Us with Brené Brown* podcast**
Conversations that focus on unlocking and exploring the deeper parts of ourselves so that we can courageously live and love authentically.

***When Things Fall Apart: Heart Advice for Difficult Times* by Pema Chödrön**
Shares wisdom on living while healing and provides guidance on working through chaos and creating action, as well as cultivating compassion and courage through pain.

***52 Lists for Calm: Journaling Inspiration for Soothing Anxiety and Creating a Peaceful Life* by Moorea Seal**
The practice of list-making can help you become calmer and better organized as you further develop your relationship with yourself.

***Nurturing Resilience* by Kathy L. Kain and Stephan J. Terrell**
A clinical road map of the complexities of early and developmental trauma and how that manifests in the body.

***Change Your Brain, Change Your Life* by Dr. Daniel Amen**
A self-help book for overall brain health and making practical changes to live a healthier and better life focusing on the mind–body connection.

# REFERENCES

Amen, Daniel G. *Change Your Brain, Change Your Life: The Breakthrough Program for Conquering Anxiety, Depression, Obsessiveness, Lack of Focus, Anger, and Memory Problems.* New York: Harmony Books, 2015.

American Psychological Association. "Contrary to Widely Held Beliefs, Romance Can Last in Long-Term Relationships, Say Researchers." *American Psychological Association*, 2009. APA.org/news/press/releases/2009/03/romance-relationships.

Brown, Brené. "The Power of Vulnerability" TED Talk. ted.com/talks/brene_brown_the_power_of_vulnerability?language=en.

Denning, Stephanie. "Oprah: The Secret to Her Success." *Forbes Magazine*, January 9, 2018. Forbes.com/sites/stephaniedenning/2018/01/08/what-makes-oprah-oprah-her-thoughts-on-her-exceptional-success/?sh=7c938a3f5a05.

Duffey, Thelma. "Living through Adversity with Self-Compassion." *Psychology Today.* Sussex Publishers, January 27, 2015. PsychologyToday.com/ca/blog/works-in-progress/201501/living-through-adversity-self-compassion.

Gómez-López, Mercedes, Carmen Viejo, and Rosario Ortega-Ruiz. "Well-Being and Romantic Relationships: A Systematic Review in Adolescence and Emerging Adulthood." *International Journal of Environmental Research and Public Health.* MDPI, July 7, 2019. ncbi.nlm.nih.gov/pmc/articles/PMC6650954/.

Gyllensten, Amanda Lundvik, Lars Hansson, and Charlotte Ekdahl. "Outcome of Basic Body Awareness Therapy. A Randomized Controlled Study of Patients in Psychiatric Outpatient Care." *Advances in Physiology*, July 11, 2009. TandFOnline.com/doi/abs/10.1080/14038109310012061.

León, Concepción de. "How to Rewire Your Traumatized Brain." *New York Times*, October 18, 2018. NYTimes.com/2018/10/18/books/review/how-to-rewire-your-traumatized-brain.html.

Limeri, Lisa B., Nathan T. Carter, Jun Choe, Hannah G. Harper, Hannah R. Martin, Annaleigh Benton, and Erin L. Dolan. "Growing a Growth Mindset: Characterizing How and Why Undergraduate Students' Mindsets Change." *International Journal of STEM Education*, July 8, 2020. link.Springer.com/article/10.1186/s40594-020-00227-2.

Morin, Amy. "How to Make Peace with Your Past." *Psychology Today*, May 10, 2020. PsychologyToday.com/us/blog/what-mentally-strong-people-dont-do/202005/how-make-peace-your-past.

Mutiwasekwa, Sarah-Len. "Self-Love." *Psychology Today*, November 12, 2019. PsychologyToday.com/ca/blog/the-upside-things/201911/self-love.

Ravishankar, Rakshitha Arni. "How to Be the Best Version of Yourself at Work." *Harvard Business Review*, February 23, 2021. HBR.org/2019/04/how-to-be-the-best-version-of-yourself-at-work.

Royden, Leah. "Does Time Really Heal All Wounds?" *Psychology Today*, May 31, 2019. PsychologyToday.com/us/blog/the-mourning-after/201905/does-time-really-heal-all-wounds.

Shetty, Jay. *Think Like a Monk: Train Your Mind for Peace and Purpose Every Day*. London: Thorsons, 2020.

Smit, Dorien, Janna N. Vrijsen, Bart Groeneweg, Amber Vellinga-Dings, Janneke Peelen, and Jan Spijker. "A Newly Developed Online Peer Support Community for Depression (Depression Connect): Qualitative Study." *Journal of Medical Internet Research*, July 12, 2021. JMIR.org/2021/7/e25917/.

Vallerand, Robert J. "The Role of Passion in Sustainable Psychological Well-Being." Psychology of Well-Being. Springer Berlin Heidelberg, March 21, 2012. SpringerOpen.com/articles/10.1186/2211-1522-2-1.

Van der Kolk, Bessel. *The Body Keeps the Score: Brain, Mind, and Body in the Healing of Trauma*. New York: Penguin, 2015.

## ACKNOWLEDGMENTS

A special thank-you to my first supporter who saw me for who I am, my late dad, Domenic. My mom, Grace, whose big heart always inspires me to help others and stay humble. My sister, Teresa, who encourages me to keep challenging myself and go bigger. My brother, Vince, for encouraging me to use my vulnerability and voice to support others. To my closest friends and family, departed and present—I'm forever grateful for our bond.

## ABOUT THE AUTHOR

**Carmela Pileggi** (she/her) is a child and youth-care practitioner and educational support specialist in Toronto, Ontario. Carmela is also DIR floor-time certified through ICDL and brain-health certified through Amen University. She received degrees in psychology (BA) from Ryerson University and in child and youth care (advanced diploma with honors) at George Brown College in Toronto. Carmela has taken her passion for mental health advocacy and her lived experience with grief and as a trauma survivor to founding Girls Gotta Heal (GGH), a platform and community supporting young people navigating grief and loss as well as rediscovering and building their relationships with themselves. GGH offers peer support and programming virtually for young women all over the world. Follow on Instagram @girlsgottaheal. Visit GirlsGottaHeal.com.

CPSIA information can be obtained
at www.ICGtesting.com
Printed in the USA
LVHW070754131122
733027LV00035B/1345